FUSEWIRE

T0314644

Ruth Padel has published two collections of poetry, and was
a prizewinner in National Poetry Competitions in 1992 and
1994. She lives in London.

On Ruth Padel's previous collections:

'The religious language . . . is a strong source of vocabulary
among the already spectacular collection in her possession.
Her work is very powerful . . . as in the stunning poem
"Harvest Moon". Many poets wait a lifetime for a poem
like this and still don't get one.' *Poetry Review*

'*Angel* has all the verbal dynamism, upended perspective
and implosive fire I look for and so rarely find in English
poetry. The inventive vocabulary, imagery and energy burn,
and energise the nerves. Great.' Jeremy Reed

'Like the best writer of fictions, Padel slides easily into the
skins of others . . .' Maura Dooley, *Acumen*

'Her sense of history, of the past intertwining with the
present, is most poignant.' *Times Literary Supplement*

'A poetic intelligence of considerable range and power.'
Cambridge Review

FUSEWIRE

Ruth Padel

Chatto & Windus
LONDON

First published in 1996

3 5 7 9 10 8 6 4 2

First published in Great Britain in 1996 by
Chatto & Windus Limited
Random House, 20 Vauxhall Bridge Road
London SW1V 2SA

Random House Australia (Pty) Limited
20 Alfred Street, Milsons Point, Sydney
New South Wales 2061, Australia

Random House New Zealand Limited
18 Poland Road, Glenfield
Auckland 10, New Zealand

Random House South Africa (Pty) Limited
PO Box 337, Bergvlei, South Africa

Random House UK Limited Reg. No. 954009

A CIP catalogue record for this book is available from
the British Library

ISBN 0 7011 6379 8

Typeset by SX Composing, Rayleigh, Essex

The Random House Group Limited supports The Forest Stewardship
Council® (FSC®), the leading international forest-certification organisation.
Our books carrying the FSC label are printed on FSC®-certified paper.
FSC is the only forest-certification scheme supported by the leading
environmental organisations, including Greenpeace. Our
paper procurement policy can be found at
www.randomhouse.co.uk/environment

Printed and bound in Great Britain by Clays Ltd, St Ives plc

For Jane Davies

ACKNOWLEDGEMENTS

Thanks to the editors of these, where some of these poems first appeared: *Critical Quarterly, Force 10, Fortnight, Harvard Review, Irish Times, Kenyon Review, London Review of Books, New Yorker, Poetry Ireland, The Printer's Devil, Southern Humanities Review, Times Literary Supplement, Verse, Yale Review; Klaonica: Poems for Bosnia*, edited by Ken Smith and Judi Benson (Bloodaxe 1993); *New Writing 4*, edited by Alan Hollinghurst and A. S. Byatt (Vintage Books 1995); the 1994 *National Poetry Competition Prizewinners' Anthology*.

Many thanks to the Arts Council of Great Britain for a Writer's Bursary which enabled this book to be completed.

Many warm thanks to Matthew; also to Chase, Laurie, Ian, Myles, and Paul.

CONTENTS

'It is a hard responsibility to be a stranger.'

John Hewitt, "The Search"

'Desire lines, desire paths – all cities have them: private routes through public spaces, rabbit-runs the townplanners can't plan for. You never know where they'll turn up.'

Vincent McCann, *Environment and Illusion: The Construction of Urban Experience*

TELL ME ABOUT IT

When they mourn you over there
the way you'd want, the way you mourn
your friends;

when they're celebrating
having loved you
in Derry, Rathmullen, wherever –

birettas, candles, Latin,
all the weavings you don't believe in
but love anyway and I'll never share

for who the hell converts to
ex-Catholic? – no one will know
someone's missing you here

for ever. Whose arms,
printed with that absolute
man's stillness

when your breath calms
into my shoulder and you fall asleep
inside me, open and close

in a foreign night round nothing.
Who misses the way
you pour loose change on the bar

in a puddle of fairytale silver
and move through the night,
through everything, curious,

mischievous as a mongoose,
and never an unkind word.
I might dream

of coming over, touching
just one friend's sleeve
to whisper

'Talk about him. A bit.
The way he was, here' –
but never do it. Instead

I'll say *Yes* in my sleep
to you. To no one. You'll put
your tongue in my mouth, deep,

the way you do,
and my eyes will open
on a dark garden. I'll wake up

touching myself for you.
The alarm will stare
venomous digits. I'll hang on

to the fragile haze
of a wine-bar
when you leant over the foreign formica,

haltering my hand within your two
like the filling in a sandwich,
sashaying the skin of each finger

down to the soft web between,
over and over, a rosary of rub
and slide, as if you could solder

me to your lifeline. As if
you could take me with you.
And I'll wish you had.

NEARLY NOT THERE

A bar in the middle of nowhere
in the middle of night

where a couple of national
anthems get booed from the back
of the two-money till

and families jive
to the electro-acoustic keyboard

of a Clerk (he lives
for this). A Clerk
to the County Court.

Then love songs from nowhere
sung in the night kitchen

to the purr of the fridge
and white chiffon, hissing
its bridal surprise

off the lake.
A stolen row-boat

complete
with two oars. Yes?
Yes. Bumped driftwood, kissing

the soft mud fringe of the shore
and that scallop of moon,

a C of wishbone
nearly not there
in the hair of sunrise.

THE LANE

When he drove off it was OK.
For hours he was still there
when she walked. Even washing plates

was a *frisson*. Every touch rooted his.
Every taste was wild raspberries
and the honey of

soft firework hedge-cuts
she left in his car,
still wet from the lane.

DEVIL'S TRILL

When she heard some boy's sonata
it was his thumb under her skin,
his butterfly breath

spinning a song about a girl
with pearl shoulders
opening the window, letting him in.

Every sound was the trill
of his tongue rooting down
to the clop of a kissing-gate –

the soft sulphur *phut* of a match-head
which holds back its strike
till it ups and dazzles the room.

WATER-DIVINER

Again? Get away.
Soft. Hard. Never let go. Never

stop talking. How can I know you?
What's knowing, when – ?

Strawberry time, head-down in
a hedge. When is your birthday?

What is it like to be
in someone else?

You earth your way
into sleep, eeling my arm

round your pelt,
knuckling my fingers in yours

like muddled electric
cable under the sea.

THE APPOINTMENT

Flamingo silk. New ruff,
the ivory ghost
of a halter. Chestnut curls,

commas behind the ear.
'Taller, by half a head,
than my lord Walsingham.'

His Devon-cream brogue,
malt eyes. New cloak
mussed in her mud.

The Queen leans forward,
a rosy envelope of civet:
a cleavage

whispering seed-pearls.
Her own sleeve
rubs that speck of dirt

on his cheek. Three thousand
ornamental fruit baskets
swing in the smoke.

'It is our pleasure
to have our servant trained
some longer time

in Ireland.' Stamp out
marks of the Irish.
Their saffron smocks.

All carroughs, bards
and rhymers. Desmonds
and Fitzgeralds

stuck on low spikes,
an avenue of heads
to the war-tent.

Kerry timber
sold to the Canaries.
Pregnant girls

hung in their own hair
on city walls. Plague
crumpling gargoyles

through Munster. 'They spoke
like ghosts crying
out of their graves.'

YOUR PLACE OR MINE?

'We go with thirteen squires.
Richard Harte of Suffolk,
income fifty pounds *per annum*,
has the papers. You're a lucky man
to get on the roll.

The soft Worcester lot
prefer Armagh.
They lay their orchards out
like dreams
of the Vale of Evesham.

We clear our virgin land of rocks
then break it,
keeping caliver and musket
primed in the last furrow
by the dribble of black trees.

We build our turrets safe
with bulls
of local granite.
For tenants, a wattled bothy.
We track the human wolves

to lairs, and terminate.
A pleasant hunt,
and fair prey falls
to the followers.'
So wrote Thos. Blennerhasset,

Norfolk squire,
pondering the limes
and wooden angels
of the church back home,
dedicating his pamphlet

to the youngest British prince,
and telling his man
to fax it
(or that's how I divine it)
thirteen times.

LETTER

'. . . and our walls took
four years. For our design
we chose a squashed ellipse –
an already battered shield
before the river.

And then four years of dust.
Of having to keep men
furnished all the time
with Corselets, Muskets,
Powder. We did our best

to make a place of Fire
a place of Law.
Stone from all over.
No Catholics within the walls.
It's for their good.

Our Quarter Sessions
stand for their defence
as well as ours.
We dispense
justice from mortar.

These are the crimes.
Ploughing by the Tail.
Selling Bread and Wine
in a Solitary Place
to Outlaws.

Refusal
to Assist our Constables
in bringing Criminals
to Jail. Poaching Salmon
or Relieving Rebels;

Acquittal
of Prisoners by Jurors.
Join me here.
This rude remote kingdom.
Such reeling times.'

THE BIGGEST FOOTPRINT

1 – *Hernán Cortés*

'The most important of their idols
in whom they have most faith

I had taken from their places
thrown down the steps
and images of Our Lady put there

which caused Montezuma
and the other natives sorrow.'

2 – *Timofeyevich Yermak*

Leading a force of eight hundred
he overthrew

the Tartar khanate of Kuchum,
opened Siberia
for Russian conquest

and blatted out
the last of the Golden Horde.

3 – *Florence von Sass-Baker*

From the White Nile, 1807.
'We are getting very short
of handkerchiefs.'

4 – *FB 477*

Our transmitter
in geo-stationary

orbit over Asia.

Whoever you are
can't escape.

MIST

Next morning the whole house swum
in it. All you could see
was the sun

rainbow-tipped as an oil-slick,
whisking a fanwheel
through the plantation,

feathers firing
on all cylinders
for a day he wasn't in.

Every tread
outside her door was his.
Tentative.

Waking her
from a sleep just begun.
As for the wild plot under her window,

foxgloves wide-open
as the Gold Pages' heading on 'Fun',
dayglo *astilbe* astir round the pond

in a shamelessly
all-pink, feathery waiting:
didn't they know it was useless?

SKIN

Remember how the screen
of your machine bruised
blue and milky as you touched it,
liquid under your fingers,

then faded as you touched
somewhere else: the whole
screen a going and coming
of bruises and fades?

HIGH-RISK COUNTRY

So I'm in love with you and it won't last?
Way of the world? These things,
you'll say on the voice-mail, pass.

But for this moment, this city I seem
to have chosen, your dreamed-against
city, the one with the name that hurts,

plus this roomful of Australian Sauterne
in paper cups, my lips open, cream-
crust broken, to drink just the thought

of you. As if hearts could turn
over without the exchange of caught
cells, this coda

of blood-tests and clinics. A mad
software breathlessness takes me apart
because your eyes are out there,

a door to look into where
I'm always lost and don't care
because you're in there too.

DESIRE PATHS OF SARAJEVO

He'd had a research project: the Indo-China *rage*.
He knew the folk-cure. A raw ruby,
the bigger the better, slung round the throat
in a pouch of salt. As near the heart as possible.

But for all his mother's lore
that started him off on this kick –
the little-sepalled rue
picked at night from ledges on Mount Belasnija –

he knew his stuff. He'd been to medical school.
Zagreb, Karachi, London. He'd been on the trail
of phibellasomes in the immune system,
suspended between two leaves of Boston glass:

his bench-space in the lab at Sarajevo.
They met in Burlington Arcade,
both window-shopping, bored, both dreaming of
impossibly sweet *raki*,

the pear *raki* you only get
from trees on Mount Igman,
served warm with *burek*
in Bas-Carsija. Later, home,

they'd joked on small salaries
about a basement in Dobjinje,
a house open to all. She had a scar now,
a strawberry sabre up her inner thigh,

where the shell
that ground her mother into their flat
had left its salt-lick. He'd sewn it –
an Oxfam needle – but rarely saw it.

Only in half hours off
the amputating table.
These August nights,
while the rest of Europe's lovers

were spotting Leonids
from windows that still had glass,
he'd lie out with her on rough ground
between burnt cars.

Noise? They hardly noticed.
He'd keep his hand still, to tease.
Three fingers in her. Sniper-fire
coding the stars.

                    *

Mostar. Ninety miles from her.
The generator
pumps flow from the Neretva,
rilling gastro-colitis

through a Braille of homes.
Nine-year-old Upha, face purple
in the basement candlelight – the hospital
they said they'd help in shifts:

her shrapnel cuts
seep rubies through her leg.
What he hangs on to is one night –
they'd still had electricity,

he'd still had a room –
when the Vice-President
howled on radio like a moonstruck wolf.
The night Sekakovic

told General Kikanjac
Go fuck himself
or he'd blow the hydro-electric plant
sky-high over Visegrad.

The night they knew
things had got mad. No backturn.
And he'd knelt up above her, parting her,
two hands in a soft karate chop,

staring in at her pink shadows
before his kiss, his tongue, her salt
became the only things.
Sea-level. A burning.

*

I thought I saw them,
standing with my safe child
on my old lover's balcony,
in a muddle of new roofs

below Mount Iouktas,
watching a near-full moon
beyond this city's wall
where Marilen and Niko

argue in whispers
over nappies unavailable
in Sarajevo.
If *this* was Mostar?

Maybe I've got it wrong.
None of us are . . .
and who's inventing who?
Imagining, all the same —

if this was us?
Your fingers and tongue
in me out there
on the rough ground

under uprooted oleanders?
Us drinking, you teasing,
in Novi Pazar,
under the pierced milk-alabaster

of the old bazaar
where pigs and geese
once fought for space,
where woodcarvings and leatherware

glowed in the black-finned lamps?
Where now old newspapers –
Oslobodenje, Le Monde,
The Herald Tribune, Al-Ahram,

Frankfurter Allgemeine Zeitung –
telling like Roman astronomers
so many coffee-cup hopes
are skittering in hot wind?

                    Heraklion
                    1993

WHEREVER YOU ARE

I imagine an office. That'd drive
me insane to start with. Investors
windowing in complaining,
brangling your name, shove

at you got-to-be-acted-on-now
memoranda. Meetings. CNN
round the clock. Tickertape
rolling mortar-attacks like water,

byline Nablus, Mogadishu, Enniskillen.
More meetings: and shouting.
I see you fluent in
chaos, lost papers, *errata*.

Wanting you happy,
I make you up in my head
like a Mozart sonata,
probably wrong: until evening

when you magnet me first to a bar
(that's easy), then, by car, back
to a house by the sea:
the full (let's say) moon

pencilling soft-glitter spoor
over home waves that keep me
(but they're only the first
thing, the tangible) away.

And I lose you
where rays from a window
bevelled for ocean light
lick granite beside a night door.

FOR SURE

I imagine a letter from you
with your r's on the outside
that will always pretend to be v's.

I buzz it out to the sun
as if it were translucent
and had to get back
to its element

but look –
I spontaneously combust
before I read
and all my curled particles

take off over the lake:
a ghostwave of filings
from burnt Melba toast.

Something, for sure,
will carry the lot of us
sizzling,
a softfall of cinders to you,

through strata
of dragonflies, sludge-piles
of minnows and slurry,
over the border no one can see,

where post-
boxes change colour
and all the distances
are miles.

EVEN THE SEA

Even the sea
she hasn't seen so long,

ten years she hasn't seen it,
the bluest eye,
a mess of cobalt,

plus the stain-blood rocks
where the same old
yellow goats flicker,

and cave-mouths
below these lover's-leap cliffs,

flushing base currents out
to a hare's-paw
of purple and silver –

even all this, she says
in her head,

is the waveline
sweat leaves between us.
What you'd do to me

if you were here:
carob-stalks

brushing iron earth
red as a setter
ruffled arse-backwards in wind

are you, so
deep I can't breathe
right down to the Y

of a tuning fork.
*What have you done
to the way I see my world?*

MRS MONTGOMERY

She's been told it's a wild place.
George holds three bishoprics.
Names I cannot remember

they are so strange. Except one.
Derry. I pray to God
it makes us all merry.

We are settled in a very
pretty house, builded of course
after the English fashion.

I told Jane, if I came here
I should be full of lice
and so I am. 'Tis true.

When Cahir
set fire to the house
he took her along with him.

Blockstraw blanching in sleet.
Banners and saffron,
a rope-trick

of goatskin. Bare legs.
She was returned unharmed
to her owner the bishop.

CONN

He gets the summons.
London parchment, Royal seal.
Let the *King* arbitrate
on rent with the O'Cahans?

If he goes
it's the Tower, no question.

These flag-green lands, his lands,
they've freebied as confetti
to his rivals. Churchmen –
Bishop Montgomery for instance –
have stolen more.
Fishing lost on the Bann.
No worship, not even in private.

The English garrison
mock him to his beard.
His men jerk-hung
to testify against him.

So pack up the bags and ride.
Ride slow, to Rathmullen

with black ballad ponies,
family, the lads. There –
connect the dots up, sixty-ton
at anchor, camouflaged with salt,
fishing nets, French flags.
Cucunnaught
disguised as a sailor, loading.

Wait. What God said to wait for –
Conn. Your man. Your son (one
of them). Conn in the hills.
All day French canvas sags.

Midnight the captain breaks,
high-tailing off the shingle,

right up the Lake of Shadows.
Or that's how I picture it
from the other sea – no right,
you'll say, to picture it at all –
what every Irish child
counts back from
and no English kid's ever known:

the nervy boat, tall cold
up and downs like a racehorse,
wind on the face, foxed gold
in a Virgin-mantle sky

staring, like every night,
like this one, down

to that silverlit foam.
'All the nobles of Tyrone,
Donegal, Fermanagh with their seed'
(except for Conn). The way ahead
a shadow of teeth to Rome
and their estates
forfeit to the London crown.

THE WAY MUD DRIES

The fields are empty
but you see
from the Ulsterbus

a boy
horizontal on his tummy

in couch grass
by the road

with Leichner No. 7 (Dark)
down to a line on his throat
one inch from the rifle-haft.

On the edge of town, past
Armagh Planetarium's bitten brick,

you find the dismantlers,
Gerry Molloy, Car Spoilers,
dismantled

and the child in the car-seat
waiting for Hula Hoops

stares from a blue Fiesta
into the gauzy flame
of morning-shopping mist,

a High Street
where there are no strangers to speak to,
his velour pajama tide-marked by

that kiss of dye
thirsting up off mum's pillow

at night when he wakes her,
and it dries the way mud dries
to a gingernut map-stain,

different loops of map each day
when she spends those five

warm seconds after waking quiet
then says Never mind
Recital Shampoo-in Colourant

Auburn to Blonde,
there's so completely nobody

she might as well be
the green plash of Bertie
Parrot on the blind.

LANDING THE GOLD

A golden eagle? *Above*
this ice-floe horizon
we were never meant to see?

While I go down
this cottonwool ski-run

whistling like a Tunnel of Love
in black and white Hitchcock

and the newcut gold twirls
of a combine harvester

on these grainlands
(red and cream as a gundog)
my eagle is leaving for ever,

plus the bump of our wheels
are you, are you in me,

the day the English girl
won a gold for hurdles

and we watched from
the wide-open bed

her flushed-up-naked surprise,
come suddenly into a great
physical inheritance.

Staggered with it.
Soft with the world.

FUSEWIRE

One double vodka. Your town,
not his. Make yourself wait
before going on

to the other pub,
the one where you'll meet.
Music? A Radio 3 quiz

and love-songs from
Azerbaijan. How weird can
you get? Where are we anyway?

How can self float
so easily
off the exact base

of the spine,
a harpsichord
magic-carpeted through mountains,

then get itself restored
by that open door in his eyes,
his tongue covering yours?

ON THE LINE

Feel, you said. *How does this feel?*
Shy, if you must know,
to be asked.

But after, when you'd left
this all-gold absence

round me, in me, in even my ears,
I wondered. Sharp,
an axe on a bell.

Blast of the *Trovatore* chorus
when you open the oven door.

An extra-terrestrial
skiffle in the dish
at Jodrell Bank.

As if I'd never known red.
Hi-volt chillies
doing press-ups in a haybag of velvet.

An anaconda with hiccups.
Like the only thing. Like you.

MR EXOCET

She dreamed
he made a scape ship
from a grandfather clock,

bone soap,
and the certainty
that human'll breed true.

Refuse the transhuman,
he'd thunder in his sleep
to the digital alarm.

But that's the old style him.
He's bought air purifiers,
banned whisky from her house,

eats only yellow food.
He's carving granite
tables of exogamy.

Marry out. Seek help from
inner cracks of outer space.
Inbreeding

blossoms the nightmare.
Together
we could be anything.

MAD DOG

1

'Why urge me on
Agamemnon?
I'm panting for it too.

I've done
what I can –
eighteen arrows glued

in young male flesh . . .
But Hector, that mad dog –
I can't get him.'

2

No one had come to tell her
he'd be outdoors tonight
in the black
beyond the city.

But they found her then alright –
indoors, working on
twizzles
of snowberry cloth

bronze tripods
spitting
behind her on the hearth
(hot baths

are the agenda when he's back)
not knowing
the time for baths,
even bloodbaths, had passed.

34

TROPICALS

He's twenty-six. Highlights.
Close-fuzz hair. Left arm
tattooed, a love-knot
of bilberry cobras, *K. A. I.*

What's – ? '"Kill. All. Irish."
They'll get me. I know that.
But I'll take a parish
with me when I go.'

In the front room, closed-circuit
hung from a meat-hook
pans empty milkjars
on the bullet-freckled porch.

In the wall his six-foot tank
of Tetra, Pink Skunk Soldier,
Coarse Wolf Eel. Torch Boy,
Snowflake Clam. Black Widow.

Under the goldleaf skitterings
she watches neo-libraries of *Morse*
on the black shammy sofa
till he's home: rear window

of the choc-ice Volvo
blooming like a pulsar
with her decoys: her scarf,
her cut-out of a Celtic left-half.

HONEY

Plastic visors
half-cock over the nose. Rifles
over each camouflaged pelvis
like a dot-dash-and-carry hose.

My countrymen. Each set of hands
in one line, the same line,
straightening the spine

of a viper between them
on Platform Four. Aliens,
trying to get a retriever,
all golden plumy shivers

to her tail, to plumb the bouquet
of each white coffin
backing every bench:

the peat-fill of bush-rose,
primula, heart's-ease
for the Belfast Central flowerbeds,
downline. She gets called back

if she skips one
or feints to the wall
where the last Lhasa Apso peed.

On the uptrain
we watch from our windows.
What was the tip-off?
Does it all depend on one dog?

CROSSED PALM

A kickstart of riverlight
along the woollen mills,
pale air-and-soapsud wharfs
where the little girl begged

by a bookshop. Empty streets,
just-out-of-bed streets,
so full of you.
(*I'll ring you tonight.*
I'll be there at two.)

If she'd said –
as blown leaves mosquito'd the river,
and I dropped silver
uselessly in to her taffeta hat –

that I'd sit like a stammer
watching me lose you
while a conference
of killer butterflies
alias dentists

swarmed over us at the bar,
that same aquarium-velvet saloon
that's been thirty
years knowing you,

a bar where you shift into shadow
away from the doorman
but crumpled your knuckles in,
fusing us under the table,
reckless in spite of your greyflower

whispering city
where everyone knows
you but not me:
I'd not have believed her.

PRIMROSE PATH

You ferried me
past peeing football fans
in Leinster Road. Rush hour

for early prostitutes:
courgette flowers
under tall histories

of building frauds
you talked of all the way.

This was like loving
a dolphin,
not knowing its range

of hideaways under the sea
or playing house in ice-shanties

on a great winter lake
before the firegrass came.
What I was hoping to say

to you. What I was hoping
you'd say —

but found myself staring instead
into octopus eyes. Not
giving anything away.

HAPPY HOUR

Greyhound your eyes
through Sierra Tequila
and Ouzo Olympia

simmering in
three yards of foreign vintage:
cream-green, parsley, ice-beige
Albanian Kristal,

Bull's Blood Glamorgan,
pomegranate, ultramarine,
Crème de Cacao de Campagne:

a rainbow of export and promise
playing the New Corfu Bar
off against old-gold mountain behind.
Only truth does? But how do you know

what that is
when you find yourself waiting
in a zoo of karaoke

for a phone to ring somewhere in Greek
through the thin foyer
from bowels of a summer hotel
with your soul (or whatever)

faxing itself
to a city of rain, moons and pubs,
newly crazed-over streets

and all so misleadingly soft
that we'll never
see something like that
in each other again?

PORTUGAL

When letters lie on the mat
with a foreign stamp up
it's nearly you. I could write it.

You won't. You've no time,
don't put anything on paper
and wouldn't want to hurt.

Instead there's a house-swap,
an invite. Someone else's place –
where we'd sift each other

over and over – think of it –
into the red, into the west
like a salt-mill that won't stop:

and in the night your fingertips
won't let mine slip
from your chest.

An almond-veiled orchard,
blazing blond town
where no one knows your face

as it keeps away the sun
but me;
and we're both foreign.

No internet. No modem,
consul, or satellite connexion.
Green hills whose hurt

doesn't matter. Whatever
it is, won't faze us.
Just history and grass.

From twelve to twelve to twelve
we let feathers of light,
cavorting up ochre-splashed walls,

make the choices for a day
where both voices are strange
but not to themselves.

A land
we have nothing to do with
mispronouncing our names

in accents we won't understand.
Somewhere neutral.
Somewhere between us, and never.

BLACK HOURGLASS

She's dressed
for her Trick or Treat do
as a badmagic nun.
Months have drowned

since she woke us at night
when she dreamed a posse of stars
flicked down, bossy frisbees,
to scalp her –

since the phone got stretched
on the carpet
next to the bed
for it might have been you.

The dog curls through the duvet,
a part-time angel
shutting his eyes
as if Trick and Treat guns

never worked. Anywhere. Anytime.
Someone
left a pink suitcase
down Carriage One? I'm back

on a train where everyone
looks up at the smallest bump.
Donabate. 'Mind the Gap'
upside-down on the kerb.

Bonfires of slack
sparkle in rice-paper smoke
on a siding. Blue Grass,
scent of my own first dance,

wafts to the edge of Newry
from the redhaired girl
hustling a child to the loo.
Lisburn: a scare on the line.

Decanted, we shiver
for coaches
in our semolina dusk.
A scare on the motorway:

I've landed a lift
with a nun (but whose nun?)
imagining you on
your Club seat to Florida,

antibiotics, 'strong ones',
loose in your raw-silk shirt
with the Gold Card,
the silver, the condoms.

ALIENS

These mainline stations
where wives deposit husbands
as if there were no mistake.

Beechleaves. Crystal
rust in a pancake of floss.
Wivelock, Three Bridges:

their sunlit cement, wet-
settling when we two
were kids in two countries

(should never have met),
now cracked
into Death Valley craters

for willowherb fluff
and red mould
fantasising

of a wonderful life
in the eyes of a potato.
I'd give all these Gold

Blend promises to hold
you again, now, naked.
Own up to the dive

of your tongue,
that stubble foxing
birthmarks into my thigh.

Watch you ferret and run
for marron silk socks in
the blur-light at five.

ARCTIC FOX

As you breathe your path
to oblivion beside me
you skelter away, closing your fur,

caulking my arm
firm round you, a melt-down
of hibernating skulls, subtle

as the choreography
of the Japanese-opera-trained
Royal Lancashire recruit,

nineteen-year-old eyes
in his camouflaged back
perfecting

that lynx-in-kidboots shuffle
down Broot-
ally road, Armagh.

'I'd be lost', you say, 'out there' –
meaning my city.
A word in your ear:

what I sent
got itself stolen.
How could all that disappear?

CONJURING TRICK

Something impossible has happened.
They wanted a mirror, those eyes,

laser moons in the storm –
and they wanted the whole storehouse.

Now they're a shield. Black ice
eyes of an evening, an enemy
holding the night sky against me.

Your flood should have made
the thing grow, not die:

a child of the night
instead of your kind goodbye.

GECKO

You wake and the warm dream sticks
like velvet. Nice. That moment

before it peels away
as a lizard sheds her tail

and you wake up to having lost
what you were so amazed to be given

and find yourself splayed
with 5p-size pearl suckers

on your fingers to the glass
it's all too easy to remember through

where someone's tears have dried
outside in running stitch.

THAT BLUE HOTEL

At breakfast the Dublin
contractor
was persuading
two well-wrapped Egyptians
to invest in Donegal farming.

'Your contact
up there's Tom Sweeney.
He'll look after you, up there.'

I wanted something innocent –
I think. One corner thirsty
for me. But you've turned
into a mogul in
the flower-sellers' wars.

Alone among cold poached egg
and wuzzled investors
plus mystic ads for the wilds of Antrim

I spot a chastity padlock –
the spooling
of liquid graphics –
a straitjacket
right round the statue

of bronze
Ariavariadadne
in the Glen of the Mad.

FOREIGN NEWS

'He uncrackles his diagram
to be put into force
the day a British audience
hears Gerry's voice.

The three bottom counties
dotted. They will be given away
so the rest
will be easier to hold.

He skims the top counties
flecked like a collie
where the minority
can be easily dealt with.

Only the centre
is lightly cross-hatched.
Here internment would cost,
and eviction gives men

to the enemy over the border,
so nullify's the choice.
This shouldn't take long.
Two weeks at most if

they're all rounded up.'
In London
I can't believe
I'm reading this.

We have a scandal here.
A minister
with illegitimate kids –
political chicks home to roost.

Is all this in Ireland
not front page till it happens?

STROKE CITY

Saturday night was silver.
Always was. Even in Derry.
Even the last

when you took me
up the steep road,
your long commute, past

fort walls and Pizza Huts
to the oldgold storybook tower.
Waves spat their fusillade

kisses-gone-wrong at our feet.
'That's where I live.
Opposite

the island. Colours fall
in the morning there – like paint.
Pity you can't see the sea.'

I've slipped from a Yule log
and cricketbat world
I can't secondguess

in your head: some fibreglass
Tudor ET ('we haven't got
rid of them yet')

out of place as a 'No Through Zone'
or the crisp-packet condoms
round barracks

in their foam of khaki mud.
'British, and cool.'
Lost, of course.

Nervous. But – *cool*?
You must be . . .
. . . for missing off 'London'

and refusing to put it back
for the cops.
Who am I to – ?

Snowblind. A luxury art-
icle. Pepper and salt in the dark.
British. Whatever that is.

SAMBUCA

We're a mistake. A folksong.
Wrong. When I'm with you now
I hand across dumb flame
all in one piece for you,
that can't give out its velvet.

We made this street our own,
breathless, or I was,
at the nuclear kiss
of your hand on my ribs
in dark summer traffic
and gunmetal Gothic
Church of Ireland shade.

But for this Christmas
dance of cold stories
we're a quick midnight
adult cartoon. Blue fire
from the surface

of *four* complimentary
liqueurs ('life's tough
at the top')
slithers between us,
sticks to your fingers,
bites when you try
to snuff it out.

COLD

You're almost fifty. Nightlong
the stubble grows white
against my throat. We unwrap

in an attic that smells of tar.
When you push inside, you keep
your eyes closed
as if there's no through way.

These blue corridors, mazy
stairlets, have lost us. We run
from one carved pub to another,

sneezing under high ceilings,
talking magic wands: your father
proud of you,
his voice a surprise through

a voice on a train. Plus
the dottiness of believing
your Church.

Talking? I listen. Hours
I hold you, stare
at the bathroom strip-glow,
one aureole of hi-glisten ivory

up the half-shut door.
This is me adrift, spindrift
in your sleep. Drowning in fog.

Learning the unearthly start of ferns,
their brittle browning back,
the many ways of leaving
your town. Where did we go?

SOME NOTES

THE APPOINTMENT

Elizabeth sent Ralegh to Ireland in 1580.

In Ireland: 'Certainly the miseries of war are never so bitter and many as when a whole nation or a great part of it forsaking their own seats labour to root out the established possessors of another land.' So wrote Ralegh when he got there, no slouch at massacres and possessions himself.

They spoke like ghosts: as Junior Secretary, after Lord Grey's 'pacification' of Munster, 1583, Edmund Spenser watched thirty thousand Irish die of plague and famine.

YOUR PLACE OR MINE?

Quotes from Mr Blennerhasset's pamphlet, titled *Direction for the Plantation of Ulster*, printed *c.*1610, dedicated to Prince Henry.

LETTER

The walls of Derry, finished in 1618, were planned as 'a distorted ellipse like a battered shield' (A.T.Q. Stevens, *The Narrow Ground: Aspects of Ulster 1609-1969*, 1977, p. 56). The city was renamed Londonderry in 1613, but the Catholic population never used that name. In 1984 the City Council voted to change the name back to Derry. The name still marks division in the population. It has been very dangerous to use the wrong name to the wrong person. You ask for a ticket to Derry and get told there's no such place. See STROKE CITY.

Crimes, Ploughing by the Tail: from Patrick Macrory, *The Siege of Derry*, p. 49.

Such reeling times: words of Robert Monro (died *c.*1680), 'zealous plunderer of many Ulster towns', according to Roy Foster, *Modern Ireland*, p. 80.

THE BIGGEST FOOTPRINT

It has been argued that the British relation to Ireland was not true colonisation. If that's right, this poem is less relevant than I thought. But from this side, British footprints in Ireland, at least till the end of the seventeenth century, do look very *like* it.

DESIRE PATHS OF SARAJEVO

Heraklion, where this poem started, was colonised by Turkey for many centuries: like Sarajevo.

MRS MONTGOMERY

'It was decided to set up an established Church, which, needless to say, was to be Protestant. Ulster till then had been less affected by the

Reformation than any other part of Ireland. It was covered by three bishoprics: Derry, Raphoe, and Clogher, the first two held by Catholic bishops till 1600. Clogher had been vacant thirty years. The three were now amalgamated. By a neat stroke of nepotism, George Montgomery was appointed to the lot. He was already rector of Chedzoy, Somerset, and dean of Norwich. His wife encouraged him to draw his bishop's emoluments without moving. But they were packed off, out of their comfortable East Anglian rectory, to Ulster.' From Macrory, *The Siege of Derry*, p. 38.

CONN

In August 1607, after thirty years fighting the British in Ulster, Hugh O'Neill, 'that damnable rebel Tyrone' (Sir John Harington called him), left Ireland for ever, and went with other Catholic nobles to Rome. His friend Cucunnaught organised the transport from Lough Swilly, 'Lake of Shadows', in Donegal. His son Conn got left behind. This was the 'Flight of the Earls', a landmark in Irish history, which left Ulster bare of Catholic leadership against the British.

Bishop Montgomery: See MRS MONTGOMERY

MAD DOG

From Homer, *Iliad*, viii. 293-9 and 23.438-45.

TROPICALS

From a 1993 interview in a London paper with an Ulster gunman, one of the men (on both sides) known as 'Mad Dog'.

BLACK HOURGLASS

In October 1993 hitmen in Hallowe'en costume machine-gunned The Rising Sun at Greysteel outside Derry, in retaliation for an IRA bomb which killed many adults and children in a fish shop.

Donabate, Newry, Lisburn: towns on the Belfast-Dublin railway line, on which bomb-scares were frequent.

FOREIGN NEWS

Plans for ethnic cleansing in Ulster were reported in London papers in 1993.

STROKE CITY

Controversial name invented by Derry newscaster Gerry Anderson to describe the dilemma of Derry (Catholic)/Londonderry (Protestant). See LETTER.

COLD

'Unearthly start of ferns': Patrick Kavanagh, *The Great Hunger*, II.